W9-AJP-891

TENNESSEE

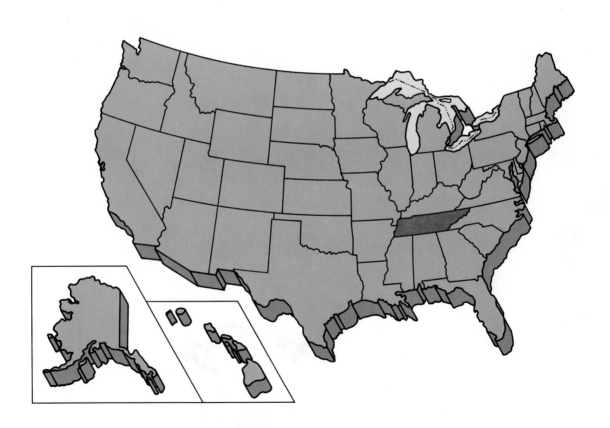

TENNESSEE

Karen Sirvaitis

Lerner Publications Company

LIBRARY OF CONGRESS
CATALOGING-IN-PUBLICATION DATA
Sirvaitis, Karen.
    Tennessee / Karen Sirvaitis.
      p.   cm. — (Hello USA)
    Includes index.
    Summary: Introduces the geography, history, people, industries, and other highlights of Tennessee.
      ISBN 0-8225-2711-1 (lib. bdg.)
    1. Tennessee—Juvenile literature.
    [1. Tennessee.] I. Title. II. Series.
    F436.3.S58   1991
    976.8—dc20   90-13533
                                              CIP
                                               AC

Cover photograph by Root Resources.

The glossary that begins on page 68 gives definitions of words shown in **bold type** in the text.

Manufactured in the United States of America

1 2 3 4 5 6 7 8 9 10 99 98 97 96 95 94 93 92 91

 This book is printed on acid-free, recyclable paper.

CONTENTS

Morris Frank from Nashville, the first American to have a Seeing Eye dog, stands with Buddy.

Did You Know . . . ?

❏ The Seeing Eye, which opened in Nashville in 1928, was the first organization in the United States to train guide dogs for blind people. Buddy, a German shepherd, was the first Seeing Eye dog.

❏ Clarence Saunders of Memphis, Tennessee, created the world's first supermarket. Saunders got the name for his market after watching a pig wiggle under a fence. He designed one long, winding aisle for the store and called it Piggly Wiggly.

☐ In 1886 Tennessee became the first state to have two brothers run against each other in an election for governor. Robert Love Taylor received more votes than his brother Alfred Alexander did, but Alfred was not to be left out. In 1920 he ran for governor again (not against his brother) and won.

☐ A temporary state called Franklin existed from 1784 to 1788 in what is now eastern Tennessee. Although Franklin, named after Benjamin Franklin, had its own constitution and governor, the state was not formally recognized by the United States. Franklin became part of Tennessee in 1796.

A Trip Around the State

Walk through Tennessee from west to east and you'll cross gently rolling hills, fertile farmland, and miles of misty mountains before completing your journey. The state has three land regions, commonly called West, Middle, and East Tennessee. Because these regions look so different, Tennessee has been described as three states in one.

Tennessee is located in the southeastern United States. Shaped almost like a rectangle, the state has two natural boundaries—the Mississippi River in the west and the Appalachian Mountains in the east. Eight states border Tennessee. They are Kentucky, Virginia, North Carolina, Georgia, Alabama, Mississippi, Arkansas, and Missouri.

Tennessee's westernmost region, called West Tennessee, is a plain with rolling hills, wide valleys, and flatlands. Two major rivers, the Mississippi and the Tennessee, fence off the plain from bordering states and from Middle Tennessee.

Middle Tennessee holds a large **basin** (a wide, bowl-shaped dip in the earth's surface). Many farmhouses and crops are found in this fertile area. **Plantations** (large farms) were once common in the basin, which has been called the Garden of Tennessee. The land along the eastern edge of the basin gradually slopes upward to meet the foothills of the Appalachian highlands.

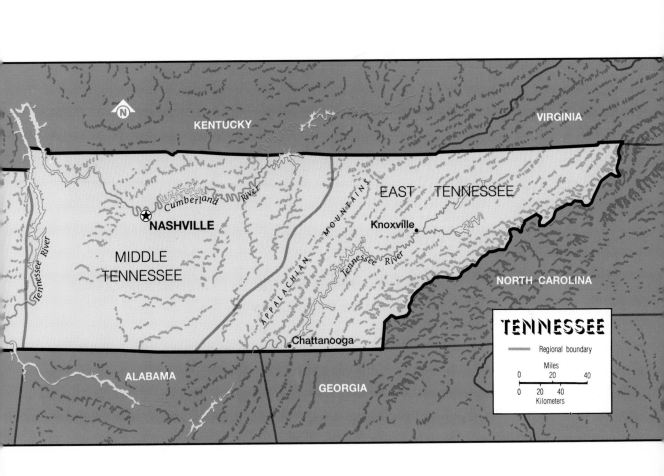

KENTUCKY

VIRGINIA

Cumberland River

★ **NASHVILLE**

Knoxville

EAST TENNESSEE

Tennessee River

MIDDLE
TENNESSEE

A P P A L A C H I A N   M O U N T A I N S

Tennessee River

NORTH CAROLINA

Chattanooga

ALABAMA

GEORGIA

TENNESSEE

Regional boundary

Miles
0   20   40

0   20   40
Kilometers

The Great Smoky Mountains, also called the Smokies, form the border between Tennessee and North Carolina.

The foothills mark the beginning of East Tennessee. A wide valley separates the foothills from the Appalachian Mountains, the old-est mountain chain in North America. These mountains rose from the earth's crust millions of years ago. Some of the major Appalachian

A bridge *(top left)* **spanning the Mississippi River connects Memphis, Tennessee, with West Memphis, Arkansas. Flaming azaleas** *(bottom left)* **adorn mountain slopes in East Tennessee.**

mountain ranges in Tennessee include the Great Smoky and the Cumberland.

Three major rivers flow through Tennessee. The Mississippi, in West Tennessee, is the longest river in the United States. The Cumberland River cuts a jagged path through the northern half of Middle Tennessee. The Tennessee River, which begins in the Appalachians, loops down through Alabama before reentering Tennessee in the west.

13

There are many lakes in Tennessee. Reelfoot, one of the state's natural lakes, was born in 1811 when an earthquake sank a large piece of forest in northwestern Tennessee. The violent trembling also forced the Mississippi River to flow backward for a short period of

The trunks of cypress trees soak in Reelfoot Lake. The trees are what remain of an old forest.

The Tennessee Valley Authority (TVA) built Norris Dam on the Clinch River, which flows into the Tennessee River. Norris Dam is 265 feet (81 meters) high and 1,860 feet (567 m) long. Its reservoir, called Norris Lake, is one of the Great Lakes of the South.

time. The river quickly flooded the sunken woodland. When the ground stopped shaking, the river returned to its course, leaving behind a large lake.

More lakes were created starting in 1933. A U.S. government organization called the Tennessee Valley Authority (TVA) began building a series of dams and locks on some of Tennessee's rivers. Each of these dams holds back water, creating a **reservoir,** or artificial lake. The dozens of reservoirs in Tennessee are known as the Great Lakes of the South.

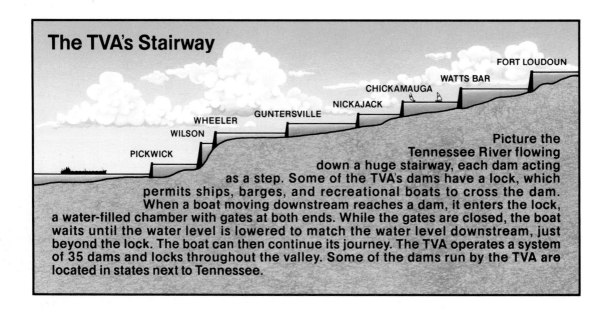

The TVA's Stairway

FORT LOUDOUN

WATTS BAR

CHICKAMAUGA

NICKAJACK

GUNTERSVILLE

WHEELER

WILSON

PICKWICK

Picture the Tennessee River flowing down a huge stairway, each dam acting as a step. Some of the TVA's dams have a lock, which permits ships, barges, and recreational boats to cross the dam. When a boat moving downstream reaches a dam, it enters the lock, a water-filled chamber with gates at both ends. While the gates are closed, the boat waits until the water level is lowered to match the water level downstream, just beyond the lock. The boat can then continue its journey. The TVA operates a system of 35 dams and locks throughout the valley. Some of the dams run by the TVA are located in states next to Tennessee.

The dams did more than create recreational lakes. They also raised the water level in shallow places, so that large ships and barges could navigate the rivers. The dams provided a cheap source of electricity for the Tennessee Valley area, and they controlled flooding caused by heavy rains.

Heavy rains do occasionally pound Tennessee, but the state's climate is generally not harsh.

Middle Tennessee gets the most rain. Throughout much of the state, snowfalls are light and the snow usually melts quickly. East Tennessee receives more snow than other parts of the state.

During the summer, temperatures average more than 80°F (27°C) in West Tennessee, the hottest region. The mountainous areas of East Tennessee are somewhat cooler. During the winter, temperatures throughout the state seldom drop below freezing.

In the spring, flowering shrubs of azalea and laurel brighten mountain slopes. Hickory, pine, oak, and poplar trees forest about half the state. The U.S. national bird, the bald eagle, nests in the forests of East Tennessee and in the marshes of Reelfoot Lake.

In the winter, great blue herons join the eagles, flocking to cypress trees that sprawl in the lake. White-tailed deer, black bears, foxes, beavers, and raccoons are also common to Tennessee.

Tennessee's Story

Little is known about the first peoples to live in Tennessee. About 14,000 years ago, Native Americans (Indians) lived in caves or camped in the woods. These people hunted, fished, and gathered strawberries and hickory nuts for food.

Eventually, the Indians began to grow their food. They planted gardens of beans, squash, and corn. They moved out of caves and used grasses and brush to build homes in villages. These Indians are known as mound builders. Some of the mound builders were expert farmers. Others were master craftspeople.

A mound builder worships a god from the top of a temple.

The mound builders are best remembered for their earthen temples and burial mounds. By hauling load after load of dirt on their backs, the mound builders eventually moved tons of soil and stones to temple sites. Some of the structures they built are still standing.

No one knows exactly what happened to these Indians, but by the mid-1500s mound building had stopped. Different Indian cultures came to the area. The Cherokee settled in the Appalachians. The Chickasaw entered West Tennessee.

The Cherokee built villages of as many as 50 log houses along rivers in the foothills of the Great Smoky

Mountains. The Cherokee were skilled hunters and farmers. Corn was their most important crop.

The Chickasaw lived near the Mississippi River, which often flooded, so they built their villages on high ground. Crops grew well in the area's rich, black soil, and the surrounding forests made excellent hunting grounds. Expert fishers, the Chickasaw often enjoyed meals of catfish.

In 1540 the Indians of Tennessee welcomed into their villages a Spaniard named Hernando de Soto. De Soto, the first European to explore what is now the southeastern United States, was searching for gold. For months he and his army

Hernando de Soto

lived among the Native Americans, who fed the newcomers and invited them to tribal celebrations.

The Spaniards did not return the Indians' kindness. When de Soto was ready to leave the area, he planned to take some Indians as slaves. Trained Indian warriors tried to stop de Soto. These Indians attacked the Spaniards, killing a great number of them.

But the Indians suffered the most. De Soto and his army had brought an enemy the Indians could not overcome—disease. By the time the Spaniards left in 1541, hundreds of Indians had died from smallpox and other illnesses.

In the following years, explorers from several European countries came to North America. To reach what is now Tennessee, some of these adventurers paddled down the Mississippi River in canoes. Others walked across the Appalachian Mountains. After these explorations, European countries claimed large regions of the continent.

Cherokee and Chickasaw lands, and areas farther east, had been claimed by Britain. The British government set up several **colonies** along the Atlantic coast in these territories. The colony of North Carolina reached inland to include all of what is now Tennessee.

By the late 1700s, colonists from North Carolina and Virginia had begun trekking over the Appalachian Mountains into what is now Tennessee. They settled in the wilderness, far from any cities, and had little or no contact with the people they left behind. The pioneers were independent. They made log cabins, horseshoes, spinning wheels, quilts, tables, chairs—almost everything they needed.

Many pioneers from the colonies traveled westward by way of the Cumberland Gap, a mountain pass in northeastern Tennessee. **Daniel Boone** (forefront) led hundreds of travelers through the passageway in the late 1700s.

23

The Appalachian tradition of making durable necessities, such as quilts, goes back to the pioneers.

To the pioneers who ventured west of the Appalachians, the Atlantic coast seemed far away. But the future of the pioneers was tied to events that were happening in the East. The British government began charging the colonists taxes on everyday items such as tea and sugar. The colonists believed the taxes were unfair.

In 1775 the angry colonists began fighting the British in a war called the American Revolution. Pioneers in what is now Tennessee were eager to go east and fight the British. But throughout the war, Tennesseans fought the Cherokee, who had sided with the British. The British had promised to help the Cherokee stop pioneers from moving onto the Indians' land.

In 1783 Britain lost the war. The 13 freed colonies formed their own nation—the United States of America. After the revolution, the Union created territories out of land that lay west of the Appalachians. A territory had less power than a state, but once it had enough people, a terri-

Some of Tennessee's pioneers lived in small settlements.

tory could become a state. In 1789 the western land that North Carolina had claimed earlier became part of the Territory of the United States South of the River Ohio.

The territory's population soon grew to more than 60,000 white people—more than enough to apply for statehood. A large chunk of the territory adopted a constitution and took the name of a Cherokee village called *Tanasie,* or Tennessee. In 1796 Tennessee became the 16th state to join the Union and the first state to be created from a U.S. government territory.

25

Ten years before Tennessee gained statehood, a boy named Davy Crockett was born in Greene County. At that time, Tennessee was the American frontier —land to which few white people had ventured.

Davy Crockett was well suited to the times. During his boyhood, he learned how to fire a hunting rifle with amazing accuracy. As a young man Crockett won hundreds of shooting contests.

Crockett used his skill with firearms to hunt bears and raccoons. He made clothing, rugs, and blankets out of the skins. He fed his family and his neighbors with the meat.

Vol.1.] "Go Ahead." [No.2.

Davy Crockett's
ALMANACK,
OF WILD SPORTS IN THE WEST,
And Life in the Backwoods.
CALCULATED FOR ALL THE STATES IN THE UNION.

1836

Col. Crockett's Method of Wading the Mississippi.

Davy Crockett loved to hunt, but he also loved to tell stories—many of them tall tales. For instance, Crockett once claimed to have killed 105 bears in one season! His friends, however, believed that Crockett was a much better storyteller than hunter.

Crockett's ability to conquer the frontier and still have a sense of humor helped to make him famous. Davy Crockett died in 1836. Since then, generations of Americans have heard his stories and have tried to understand what it would be like to be a pioneer—a pioneer in Tennessee.

While Tennesseans were settling into statehood, the United States entered into another war with Britain. The War of 1812 was fought over trading rights. The U.S. government asked citizens to volunteer as soldiers, and thousands of Tennesseans signed up to fight. This enthusiasm earned Tennessee the nickname the Volunteer State.

One volunteer was Andrew Jackson. General Jackson led a successful attack against the British during the Battle of New Orleans. Jackson became a hero. His popularity swept across his home state of Tennessee, and he decided to run for president. He was elected in 1828 and became the country's first president from the West.

Tennesseans boasted that Andrew Jackson was the first U.S. president born in a log cabin, not on a rich plantation as previous presidents had been.

Jackson served in the White House for eight years. During his presidency, settlers demanded more Indian land. Jackson believed that Americans and Native Americans could not live together peacefully. In 1830 he approved the Indian Removal Act. This law stated that Indians living east of the Mississippi River would have to move to Oklahoma, a territory west of the river.

The Indian Removal Act broke many **treaties** the U.S. government had made with the Native Americans. In 1838 the Chickasaw and most of the Cherokee were forced to walk to Oklahoma. So many Indians died from hunger and disease that the journey is called the Trail of Tears.

Under orders from the U.S. government, thousands of Indians walked the Trail of Tears. Most of these Indians were Cherokee, Chickasaw, Choctaw, Creek, or Seminole. These groups were known by white settlers in the 1800s as the Five Civilized Tribes.

Members of the Five Civilized Tribes adopted the life-style of the white settlers. Some of these Indians went to church and owned plantations. But white people wanted the Indians' land, no matter how much the Indians tried to fit in and keep peace. On the Trail of Tears, the people of the Five Civilized Tribes realized they had given up their traditions only to have to give up their homes and, in many cases, their lives.

29

This stamp advertises the services of slave traders in the 1850s.

Once the state's Indians were gone, Tennesseans had the land they wanted. But another conflict was brewing. During the 1800s, many slaves were brought to Tennessee from Africa. The Northern states had already outlawed slavery. In most of the South, however, plantation owners still found it necessary to use slaves to make a profit.

Other Southern states depended on slaves more than Tennessee did. When the U.S. government threatened to end slavery across the nation, some of these states decided to leave the Union. They formed a new country—the Confederate States of America. In the Confederacy, slavery was legal.

The Battle of Shiloh, named after a church on the battlefield, occurred in 1862 in West Tennessee. About 24,000 soldiers died or were injured in the fighting. The Union army won the battle and gained control of the Mississippi River as far south as Memphis.

Many Tennesseans were against slavery. They voted to stay in the Union. But when Abraham Lincoln, then president of the United States, sent troops to the South in 1861, Tennesseans immediately offered to help the Southern cause. Volunteers from the state lined up to fight against the North.

The Civil War had begun. Tennessee was hit hard and fast by Union troops. Forts Henry and Donelson near Nashville were taken in 1862, while they were still under construction. Before long, Union forces took the city of Memphis in the Battle of Shiloh, one of the bloodiest of the war.

31

The Union controlled Tennessee but not without a struggle. Confederate soldiers often attacked Union holdings, attempting to regain control. The fighting was fierce and frequent. Of all the states, only Virginia saw more battles than Tennessee did.

The Civil War ended in 1865. The slaves had been freed, but they, along with other Southerners, still faced many hardships. Tennessee's crops and orchards had been burned. Its farms and mansions were destroyed. Many Tennesseans had lost their lives.

During a period called **Reconstruction**, the U.S. government began to rebuild the South. Northerners also made laws to readmit

For decades after the Civil War, loads of lumber were taken from East Tennessee to help rebuild the South.

Confederate states to the Union. On July 24, 1866, Tennessee, the last state to leave the Union, became the first state allowed to rejoin.

While Tennessee's farmers were starting to grow crops again, more and more factories were being built. By the early 1900s, many Tennes-

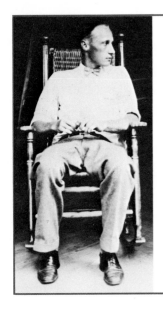

The Monkey Trial

Tennessee gained worldwide attention during the Scopes trial of 1925. John Thomas Scopes was a teacher in Dayton, Tennessee, who taught his high-school class that human beings developed from primates, which include monkeys and apes.

Not everybody agreed with this scientific point of view, known as the theory of evolution. At the time, discussing evolution in a public school was illegal in Tennessee because the belief went against the teachings in the Bible. John Scopes was arrested.

Scopes's case was tried in court and became known around the world as "The Monkey Trial." The judge said Scopes was guilty and had to pay a $100 fine to the state. Later, however, the decision was reversed. Tennessee changed the law in 1967, making it legal to teach evolution in the classroom.

seans were moving off their farms and into the state's cities to find work in manufacturing.

By the 1930s, jobs were hard to find because of a major slump in the country's economy. But in 1933, the Tennessee Valley Authority (TVA) began building dams, creating jobs for hundreds of Tennesseans. Although the TVA employed many of the jobless, it also upset many people.

For the dams to be built, some Tennesseans had to move off land their families had lived on for years. Farmhouses were torn down. Water from the dams' reservoirs permanently flooded these properties. Despite many arguments against the dams, the projects were completed. The TVA now operates 35 dams within the Tennessee Valley.

Before the TVA's dams were built, uncontrolled flooding was common in Tennessee.

Chickamauga Dam was completed in 1940 in Hamilton County, Tennessee. Gates to the dam's lock open to allow ships and freighters to pass.

The Ku Klux Klan (KKK) is an organization that started in Pulaski, Tennessee, after the Civil War. The KKK is sometimes violent toward black people and other groups whose beliefs differ from those of the Klan.

In the 1950s and 1960s, the state faced new challenges. Tennessee as well as other states experienced unrest among the country's African Americans. Black people wanted the same **civil rights** (personal freedoms) as white people. Many Americans protested laws that treated blacks unfairly.

Some protests in Tennessee were peaceful. Others became violent. Martin Luther King, Jr., was a civil-rights leader who wanted people to protest peacefully. While visiting Memphis in 1968, King was shot and killed. His death sparked several riots. In that same year, the government passed a new civil-rights law that treated blacks and other minorities more fairly.

Struggles between blacks and whites and Indians and pioneers are not far in Tennessee's past. Tennesseans now strive to make their state a place where all people are welcome to live and work.

Knoxville, Tennessee, hosted the 1982 World's Fair.

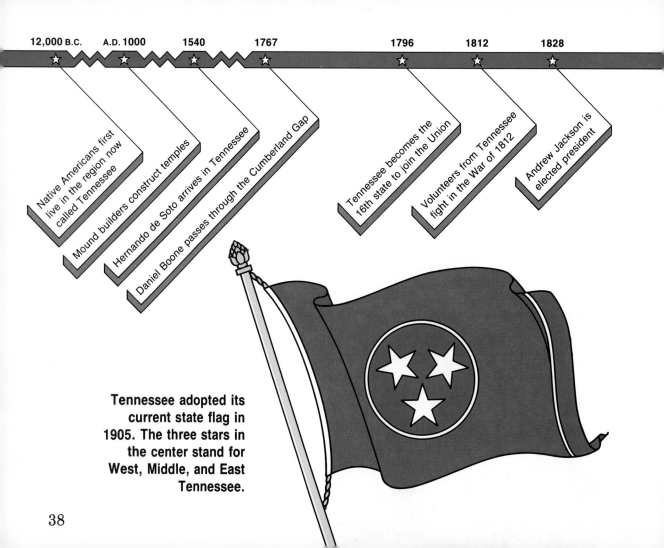

12,000 B.C.   A.D. 1000   1540   1767   1796   1812   1828

Native Americans first live in the region now called Tennessee

Mound builders construct temples

Hernando de Soto arrives in Tennessee

Daniel Boone passes through the Cumberland Gap

Tennessee becomes the 16th state to join the Union

Volunteers from Tennessee fight in the War of 1812

Andrew Jackson is elected president

Tennessee adopted its current state flag in 1905. The three stars in the center stand for West, Middle, and East Tennessee.

38

1861

Tennessee joins the Confederacy in the Civil War

1933

TVA begins building dams

1982

Knoxville hosts the World's Fair

Tennessee's state capitol building, in Nashville, is well lit after dark.

Living and Working in Tennessee

Tennessee has grown to be much different from the Cherokee village after which it is named. Most of the Indians are gone. Also gone are the days when Tennessee's pioneers settled miles and miles away from their neighbors. The state now has about five million people.

At many festivals in Tennessee, musicians entertain audiences by playing country music.

Tennesseans come from several different ethnic and racial backgrounds. Ninety-nine percent of Tennessee's people were born in the United States, and nearly half the state's residents are of British descent. Many British Americans in the Appalachians are descendants of the first white settlers to come to the area. Most of the recent **immigrants** (newcomers) are from Germany.

Roughly 16 percent of Tennessee's population is black. Other minority groups are much smaller, together making up less than 1 percent of the population. Only about 5,000 Tennesseans have Native American blood.

A small number of Tennesseans make a living just as their ancestors did—by farming the land. Only 6 percent of all working Tennesseans have jobs in agriculture, but these few grow a lot of food. Farmland covers nearly half of Tennessee. Livestock farmers raise cattle, hogs, and sheep throughout Middle Tennessee, where much of the land is good for grazing.

Soybeans and tobacco, the state's most important crops, grow in East and Middle Tennessee. Cotton,

Tennessee is a leading producer of tobacco in the United States.

Tennessee's third most valuable harvest, grows best in the climate and soil of West Tennessee. Tomatoes, snap beans, cabbages, apples, peaches, and strawberries are raised throughout the state.

Sheep graze on Tennessee's plentiful grasses.

This factory in Kingsport, Tennessee, makes chemicals and plastics.

Manufacturing employs about 25 percent of Tennessee's work force. Many factory employees make chemical products, such as paints, medicines, and soaps. Other people work with food products in meat-packing plants or canning factories. Miners dig for

44

Workers assemble new cars at the Saturn plant in Spring Hill, Tennessee.

several minerals, including zinc. The state leads the country in the production of zinc.

More than half of Tennessee's workers hold service jobs. Services includes jobs as politicians, teach-ers, bankers, salesclerks, and doc-tors. Most people who have service jobs live and work in Tennessee's cities. The largest cities in the state are Memphis, Nashville, Knoxville, and Chattanooga.

Tourists in Memphis can cruise the Mississippi River on a paddle wheeler.

Memphis, in West Tennessee, is the state's largest city. The city's hospitals, along with its many health-care professionals and research scientists, help make health care the leading industry in Memphis.

Beale Street, in Memphis, is known as the home of blues music. Memphis was also the home of Elvis Presley, a singer who since the 1950s has been called the King of Rock and Roll. Presley died in 1977, but his mansion, Graceland, is visited by more than a half-million fans every year.

A stroll down Beale Street will lead you past restaurants, shops, and nightclubs.

47

Opryland, U.S.A., the only musical show park in the country, stages 12 different performances daily.

Music is also big business in Middle Tennessee. Nashville, the state's capital, is the home of country music. A section of the city is called Music Row. Dozens of music publishing companies and recording studios line the district's 14 blocks. The Grand Ole Opry House, a theater and the world's largest broadcasting studio, lies just outside of Nashville in Opryland, U.S.A.

The Parthenon *(above)* in Nashville was built to look exactly like the ancient temple in Athens, Greece, that goes by the same name. The Old Mill Scream *(right)* is one of the many exciting rides at Opryland, U.S.A.

Tennessee walking horses often compete in horse shows.

Middle Tennessee is also famous for the Tennessee walking horse. This saddle horse is bred near Nashville. Because of their graceful step, Tennessee walking horses are comfortable to ride and are popular at horse shows.

The people of East Tennessee are proud of their history. The Museum of Appalachia in Norris displays animal traps, butter churns, wagons, gourds (used as ladles), and hundreds of other items made by Tennessee's pioneers. Each October the museum sponsors the Tennessee Fall Homecoming. At this event, visitors can experience pioneer life by boiling molasses, driving oxen, or sewing quilts.

At the Museum of Appalachia, a worker demonstrates how to plow a field the old-fashioned way—with a mule pulling a hand plow.

Some Cherokee Indians who still live in Tennessee dress in traditional clothing on special occasions.

Great Smoky Mountains National Park stretches across the border from Tennessee into North Carolina. Those who trek through this park can easily imagine what the first pioneers faced. Visitors camp in the woods, surrounded by ancient hardwood and red spruce forests. Each year, about nine million people come to this wilderness, making it one of the most visited national parks in the United States.

Just outside Great Smoky Mountains National Park lies Gatlinburg. Nestled up against the Appalachian Mountains, Gatlinburg gets enough snow to attract skiers and is one of the southernmost ski resorts in the country. This quaint Appalachian town also features hundreds of shops that sell quilts, tinware, and other crafts—items once made by Tennessee's pioneers.

The striking Great Smoky Mountains attract tourists to Tennessee.

Protecting the Environment

The Appalachian Mountains in Tennessee once looked quite different. They were taller and had sharper peaks. But over millions of years, wind and rain have been working away at the mountains, wearing them down to their present height. The process of wearing away mountains and other parts of the earth's surface is called **erosion**.

Rain and wind cause erosion of land all over the world. People in Tennessee are concerned about the erosion of one surface in particular—soil. Soil erosion can be a threat to the food supply.

Heavy rains pounding on unprotected soil can create deep gullies *(left)*—a sign of severe soil erosion. Runoff carries dirt *(facing page)* into rivers, making them muddy.

When soil erosion occurs naturally it is usually a very gradual process. As rain falls, some of it collects on the ground and flows across the earth's surface. The flowing rainwater, called runoff, carries loose soil into rivers and lakes. Over the years, runoff can carry tons of soil to a body of water. Soil erosion becomes a problem when people accelerate, or speed up, this naturally slow process.

Most accelerated soil erosion in Tennessee occurs on farmland, which covers about half the state. To prepare their lands for crops, farmers clear off the trees and grasses. The soil is then ready for planting, but it is also left unprotected from rain and wind.

For a crop to be healthy, it needs the nutrients found in topsoil.

Because Tennessee has so much cropland, a lot of soil is eroding quickly. If this rate of erosion continues, the rich **topsoil** on which Tennesseans depend to grow food will disappear into rivers and lakes.

To help save soil from erosion and to protect precious farmland, the U.S. government passed a law called the 1985 Farm Bill. To meet the goals of this law, farmers in Tennessee and other states have been reducing the amount of soil lost to erosion each year.

Farmers use several methods to slow down erosion. **Crop rotation,** or changing the types of crops planted every few years, helps keep the soil rich. When the same crops are planted year after year, they rob the soil of nutrients.

Another way to reduce soil erosion is to plant trees on farmland whose soil has become too poor to grow crops. The leaves of a tree act as an umbrella, protecting soil from harsh rains. A tree's roots help to hold soil in place. Trees and other plants also absorb rainwater, reducing runoff.

Many of Tennessee's farmers have started to practice what is called **conservation tillage**. After a crop has been harvested, farmers leave the dying plants to cover the soil, protecting it from wind and rain. When they are ready to plant again, farmers use a machine to drill holes for the seeds. The ground is not plowed, and the old, decaying crop continues to protect and add nutrients to the soil.

Trees protect soil from erosion.

Tennessee's farmers want to reduce soil erosion in their state by 50 percent, but their goal could be much higher. Farmers do not practice some of the best conservation methods because they are too costly. These methods include contour plowing and terracing, two special ways to structure a field to reduce runoff.

Tennessee has at least one resource that is needed to reduce soil erosion—people. Hundreds of Tennesseans have volunteered to save their state's soil. Once again, Tennessee is living up to its nickname—the Volunteer State.

Food grown in Tennessee stocks grocery shelves *(above)* throughout the state. To make sure enough food reaches grocery stores in the future, farmers *(right)* are changing the way they plant and harvest crops.

Tennessee's Famous People

ACTORS

Minnie Pearl (born 1912) was named Sarah Colley at birth. A comedienne, Pearl always appeared on television wearing a straw hat with its price tag dangling from the brim.

Cybill Shepherd (born 1950), from Memphis, was named for her grandfather Cy and her father, Bill. She played a leading role in the 1971 film *The Last Picture Show.* In 1990 she starred in the film's sequel, *Texasville.* Shepherd costarred in the popular television series "Moonlighting."

▲ CYBILL
SHEPHERD

◀ MINNIE PEARL

▲ LYNN SWANN

ATHLETES

Oscar Robertson (born 1938), a basketball player, was raised in Charlotte, Tennessee. In his 14 years as a professional basketball player with the Cincinnati Royals and the Milwaukee Bucks, Robertson averaged more than 25 points per game.

Lynn Swann (born 1952) brought excitement to many Super Bowl games while playing with the Pittsburgh Steelers. Swann, who was born in Alcoa, Tennessee, set many records and was named to the Pro Football Hall of Fame. After retiring from football, he became an announcer for ABC Sports.

Dragging Canoe (1730–1792) led a band of Cherokee Indians called the Chickamauga. Dragging Canoe refused to sign treaties with white people and fought pioneers who were moving into the Tennessee Valley.

Sam Houston (1793–1863) settled in Maryville, Tennessee, when he was 13 years old. At times he lived with Cherokee Indians. He later became a congressperson and then governor of Tennessee. Houston used his political position and his understanding of Indian affairs to help Native Americans.

Sequoyah (1770–1843) was a Cherokee Indian born in Tuskegee, Tennessee. He invented the first alphabet for an Indian language. Among his people, Sequoyah was honored for his leadership. The California redwood tree carries his name.

SAM HOUSTON ▶

◀ SEQUOYAH

▲ W. C. HANDY

◀ ARETHA FRANKLIN

MUSICIANS

Aretha Franklin (born 1942), known as the Queen of Soul, is originally from Memphis. As a child, Franklin began singing in the church her father pastored. Her hit records have sold millions of copies.

W. C. Handy (1873–1958) introduced a new form of music (the blues) on Beale Street in Memphis in the early 1900s. Handy, who moved to Tennessee in 1905, wrote hits such as "Memphis Blues" and "St. Louis Blues."

Dolly Parton (born 1946) sings and writes country and pop-rock music. She grew up in Locust Ridge, Tennessee, and went on to Nashville to become a star. Parton has also acted in several movies, including *Nine to Five* and *Steel Magnolias*.

Elvis Aaron Presley (1935–1977) was a legendary rock-and-roll singer. Born in Mississippi, Presley moved with his family to Memphis at the age of 13. His hit songs include "Hound Dog" and "Love Me Tender." During his career, Presley sold millions of records and acted in dozens of movies.

▲ DOLLY PARTON   ▲ ELVIS PRESLEY

◀ JULIAN BOND

DAVY CROCKETT ▼

◀ JOHN SEVIER

POLITICIANS

Julian Bond (born 1940) is a civil-rights leader and politician from Nashville. In 1968, while serving as a congressperson, Bond became the first black person to be nominated for the office of vice president of the United States.

Davy Crockett (1786–1836), who was born in Greene County, Tennessee, became a legend of the American frontier. The frontiersman, militiaman, and politician lived an extraordinary life before being killed at the Alamo during the fight for Texas's independence.

Estes Kefauver (1903–1963) was a U.S. senator who became a candidate for vice president in the 1956 presidential election. Kefauver, from Madisonville, Tennessee, is often remembered for the coonskin cap he sometimes wore.

John Sevier (1745–1815) was governor of Tennessee several times. He also served four terms in Congress and helped to make Tennessee a state.

64

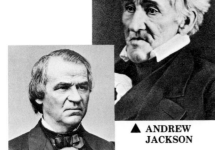

▲ ANDREW
JACKSON

◄ ANDREW JOHNSON

U.S. PRESIDENTS

Andrew Jackson (1767–1845) visited Middle Tennessee as a young man and decided to stay. He helped Tennessee become a state, and some believe he suggested that Tennessee be its name. Jackson, nicknamed "Old Hickory," was president from 1829 to 1837.

Andrew Johnson (1808–1875) was governor of Tennessee and then vice president of the United States. Johnson became president after President Abraham Lincoln was assassinated in 1864.

James Knox Polk (1795–1849) settled with his family in Maury County, Tennessee, when he was 11 years old. After serving as governor of Tennessee, Polk was elected president of the United States in 1844. During Polk's presidency, much of the West became part of the United States.

JAMES POLK ►

WRITERS

Alex Haley (born 1921) grew up in Henning, Tennessee, listening to tales of his African ancestry. He used the clues in these stories to find his family roots in a village in West Africa. After 12 years of research, Haley wrote the best-selling book *Roots*, which was made into a popular television miniseries.

John Crowe Ransom (1888–1974) was a poet and critic born in Pulaski, Tennessee. He believed that people could be happy only by leading a simple life. His volumes of poems include *Poems about God, Chills and Fever,* and *Grace after Meat.*

▲ ALEX HALEY

Facts-at-a-Glance

Nickname: Volunteer State
Song: "Rocky Top"
Motto: Agriculture and Commerce
Tree: tulip poplar
Flower: iris
Bird: mockingbird
Animal: raccoon

Population: 4,972,000 (1990 estimate)
Rank in population, nationwide: 16th
Area: 42,114 sq mi (109,075 sq km)
Rank in area, nationwide: 34th
Date and ranking of statehood:
  June 1, 1796, the 16th state
Capital: Nashville
Major cities (and populations*):
  Memphis (652,640), Nashville (473,670),
  Knoxville (173,210), Chattanooga (162,170),
  Clarksville (60,730), Jackson (52,810)
U.S. senators: 2
U.S. representatives: 9
Electoral votes: 11

Places to visit: Dollywood in Pigeon Forge, Graceland in Memphis, Great Smoky Mountains National Park in East Tennessee, Lookout Mountain near Chattanooga

Annual events: Reelfoot Eagle Watch Tours in Tiptonville (January), Great River Carnival in Memphis (May–June), International Country Music Fan Fair in Nashville (June), International Grand Championship Walking Horse Show in Shelbyville (Aug.–Sept.), National Storytelling Festival in Jonesborough (Oct.)

*1986 estimates

66

Average January temperature: 38° F (3° C)   **Average July temperature:** 78° F (26° C)

Natural resources: soil, water, marble, limestone, zinc, coal, petroleum, natural gas

Agricultural products: beef and dairy cattle, hogs, sheep, soybeans, tobacco, cotton, strawberries, apples, peaches

Manufactured goods: chemicals, food products, machinery, transportation equipment, clothing

ENDANGERED SPECIES
Mammals—mountain lion, Carolina northern flying squirrel, gray bat
Birds—Bachman's sparrow, bald eagle, common raven, peregrine falcon, interior least tern
Fish—lake sturgeon, muskellunge, yellowfin madtom
Plants—glade onion, Cumberland sandwort, Tennessee milk-vetch, heart-leaved paper birch

WHERE TENNESSEANS WORK
Services—50 percent
(services includes jobs in trade; community, social, & personal services; finance, insurance, & real estate; transportation, communication, & utilities)
Manufacturing—25 percent
Government—15 percent
Agriculture—6 percent
Construction—4 percent

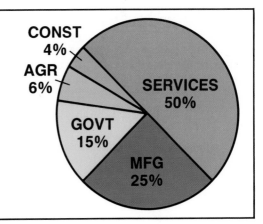

CONST 4%
AGR 6%
GOVT 15%
SERVICES 50%
MFG 25%

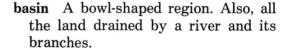

PRONUNCIATION GUIDE

Appalachian (ap-uh-LAY-chuhn)

Chattanooga (chat-uh-NOO-guh)

Cherokee (CHEHR-uh-kee)

Chickamauga (chick-uh-MAW-guh)

Chickasaw (CHIHK-uh-saw)

Choctaw (CHAHK-taw)

de Soto, Hernando (dih SOH-toh, hehr-NAHN-doh)

Knoxville (NAHKS-vihl)

Mississippi (mihs-uh-SIHP-ee)

Seminole (SEHM-uh-nohl)

Shiloh (SHY-loh)

basin A bowl-shaped region. Also, all the land drained by a river and its branches.

civil rights The right of all citizens—regardless of race, religion, sex—to enjoy life, liberty, property, and equal protection under the law.

colony A territory ruled by a country some distance away.

conservation tillage Any method of plowing and tending fields that reduces the loss of soil and water on farmland.

crop rotation Alternating the types of crops grown in a field from one year to the next so that minerals taken from the soil by one type of crop can be replaced.

erosion The wearing away of the earth's surface by the forces of water, wind, or ice.

immigrant A person who moves into a foreign country and settles there.

plantation A large estate, usually in a warm climate, on which crops are grown by workers who live on the estate. In the past, plantation owners often used slave labor.

Reconstruction The period from 1865 to 1877 during which the U.S. government brought the Southern states back into the Union after the Civil War. Before rejoining the Union, a Southern state had to pass a law allowing black men to vote. Places destroyed in the war were rebuilt and industries were developed.

reservoir An artificial lake where water is collected and stored for later use.

topsoil The surface layer of dirt in which plants grow.

treaty An agreement between two or more groups, usually having to do with peace or trade.

Index

Acknowledgments:

Maryland Cartographics, Inc., pp. 2–3, 10–11; Great Smoky Mountains National Park, pp. 2–3, 13 (bottom), 32, 53; The Seeing Eye, Inc., p. 6; Jack Lindstrom, p. 7; Frank Denobriga, Kingsport Convention and Visitors Bureau, pp. 8–9; Lynn Troy Maniscalco, pp. 9, 24; Jeff Greenberg, pp. 13 (top), 42, 43, 47, 52; Tennessee Tourist Development, pp. 12, 14, 17, 41, 54, 71; Mary A. Root/Root Resources, p. 15; Laura Westlund, p. 16, 38; Dwight Barnett, Tennessee Division of Forestry, pp. 18, 59; Tennessee State Museum, detail of a painting by Carlyle Urello, p. 19; Tennessee State Museum, from a painting by Carlyle Urello, p. 20; Library of Congress, pp. 21, 26, 31, 33, 34, 36, 63 (top right), 65 (top right and left, bottom left); Washington University Gallery of Art, p. 23; Cumberland Gap National Historic Park, p. 25; The Hermitage: Home of Andrew Jackson, Nashville, TN, p. 27; Woolaroc Museum, Bartlesville, Oklahoma, pp. 28–29; Tennessee State Museum, pp. 30, 63 (bottom right), 64 (bottom); Chattanooga-Hamilton County Bicentennial Library, p. 35; Knoxville Convention and Visitors Bureau, p. 37; Philip Wright/Visuals Unlimited, p. 39; Lisa Green, p. 40; Eastman Chemical Company, p. 44; Saturn, p. 45; D. Donne Bryant/Root Resources, p. 46; Opryland, U.S.A., Inc., p. 48; Nashville Area Chamber of Commerce, p. 49 (left); Donnie Beauchamp, Opryland, U.S.A., p. 49 (right); Voice of the Tennessee Walking Horse, p. 50; Robin Hood, Museum of Appalachia, Norris, Tennessee, pp. 51, 69; U.S. Army Corps of Engineers, Memphis District, p. 55; USDA-SCS, pp. 56, 58, 61 (right); Tim McCabe/USDA-SCS, p. 57; Karen Sirvaitis, pp. 60–61; Jim Halsey Co., Inc., p. 62 (top left); Hollywood Book & Poster Co., p. 62 (top right); Pittsburgh Steelers, p. 62 (bottom); Atlanta Historical Society, p. 63 (top left); Atlantic Records Corp., p. 63 (bottom left); David Gahr, p. 64 (top left); Independent Picture Service, p. 64 (top right); Orrin N. Alt Photography, p. 64 (center left); Archives Division—Texas State Library, p. 64 (center right); Alex Gotfryd, p. 65 (bottom right); Jean Matheny, p. 66.